STREAM OF
CONSCIOUSNESS

STREAM OF CONSCIOUSNESS

Anthony P Prior

I, Anthony P. Prior, have written the book, 'Stream of Consciousness'.

To the best of my knowledge and in good faith, this is all my own original work of creative literature.

I expect my unique style to be respected forthwith.

FIRST EDITION

TONY PRIOR ART

978-1-80227-983-2 (paperback)
978-1-80227-984-9 (ebook)

HOW TO READ JAMES JOYCE

His introspective analysis of English language,
An inquiry enquiry inquisitive enquiring into
Words representing different meanings,
But sounding the same, often, humour
Humorously humours the reader,
Repeating, replicating, subversive,
Taking the piss out of said juxtapositions,
Once sent up it comes down to representation,
Which I find fluctuating, fascinating, influencing,
You must get the joke, the contradiction,
Otherwise, it's on you misunderstanding.
Deliberate disfunctional describing,
Dissolute, desolated, dissolved dissolution,
Making no contribution to wordy revolution,
Joyce wanted to outspeak Shakespeare
And his clever plays, King Lear, no fear,
Rhythm and metre sing-along singsong,
Words all aplomb care to carry a conundrum,
Contradiction considerately considered,
Influences the outcome outpouring out.
Sing about a contrary forthwith fairy.

ALL ROADS

By definition, all roads link back to poetry,
Lyrical narrative essays, descriptive prose.
In analysis, the poetry genre and category would cover
My writing, its metre, lyricism, criticism, evaluation,
Abbreviation, consolation, revelation, understanding,
Commanding, demanding, evolving resolutely,
Punctuation fluctuation, absolution derogation,
Bearing no relation to impoverished conclusion,
Not a dead-end moribund conciliatory category,
Inflammatory, regulatory regulations regulating,
Progress nonetheless, countless times remind
Of a time when things were better previously.
Hindsight concludes retribution, revolution,
All said and done, conundrum correlation,
Hazard a guess, nonetheless confess,
Contribution to evaluation, deregulating,
Perfecting, simulating interrogating to
Find out by discrimination against
Incorrect personification of dialect,
Misdirected improper stopper stopped.

INTRODUCTION PREFACE

Anthony Prior, Writing
Poetry, Lyrical Essays.
I have a unique style,
Acquired taste,
Linguistic
Anomaly,
Analysing
My obsession with words,
Control of order,
Meaning misdemeaning,
Satisfy pleasing,
Lyrical metre,
Long and short,
Insist report,
Conclude, deduce,
Access analytical,
Logical logistical,
Summarise surmise,
Precise, abridge,
Concise, considerate,
Affirm affirmative,
Directive direct.

CONTENTS

ADOLESCENT MISSPENT YOUTH

(In Short: Disturbed, Perturbed)

Tormented by memories of stupid behaviour;
In hindsight, I would have done things differently.
Now a wise old dog with new tricks,
Complicit behaviours done to a tee, Anthony.
Commonality befriending friends with my wife,
Sugar and spice; all things nice trice.
Curb direct criticism, derogatory spite,
That trips off my tongue too easily.
I am flippant, perverse, which makes things worse
Before they've got better to the letter.
Condescend, apprehend, defend,
Disproportionate rights and wrongs,
All said and done, winding up, not down,
A stupid boy far too clever for his own good.
So, I'm told on returning retort belligerent,
Curse levelling the score flippant,
Holding no prisoners or glib protesters Protestant,
Catholic, easygoing, disobeying, conforming,
Protracted protractions, protractor setting
Unusual angles defying circumspect direct.
Granted, apologetic, non-conformity offering,
Unconventional ways to oblige disparage.

In a haze of victorious argumentative,
Pernicious spitting while swearing,
He'll leave forthwith in his disabled
Wheelchair down the road, imploding,
Exploding temper that can't be tempered.
Vile words not remembered, cursed be,
Upon the unconformity irrationally.
Disturbed foolish fool dribbles drool,
As an old tramp would misunderstand.
If only he could pretend everything was all right,
He didn't know where he would
Sleep tonight; park bench frequent,
If the smartarse delinquents would allow,
Beg, steal, borrow, the good Lord's furrow.
Live life not tomorrow, drink problem an,
Alkies life bum around beggar turned,
Out to be me drinking uncontrollably,
Like a fish, regardless of conformality.
Under duress, convicted criminality,
Delinquency, favourite, fortunate fortune,
Playing the same tune over and over,
Until people started throwing coins,
Demanding more encores, play it again,
You played it for him, now me, controversy.
Happy, spirit-based don't care,
Down more till I hit the floor.
Fully absorbed by the quart,

Delinquents perchance,
No romance, pants dance,
Give a half-chance glance,
Desire romantic romance.

Consider, considerate,
Considerable consumer,
Humour him needed,
Greed is prevalent to fill.
Stomached what he could,
Stomach wanting more,
Until his stomach ached.

Contemplate on the plate,
Ate until too late to dissipate.

Controversy plain to see,
Debauchery, wicked calamity.
The problem started as a student,
Too much freedom granted,
Friends spend who's round,
Compounded, heightened, blighted.

All right, mate, same again tonight,
Not going to drink so much this time,
Waking the neighbourhood with "Auld Lang Syne",
Hurled abuse, "No fun, drunken bum!"

Controversy accepted, rejected,
A student; what do you expect?
Free ranger slurred, suspect dialect,
Coming into effect, detect helplessness.

Dependent adolescent, drunken oblivion,
Main goal scored, abhorred.
Don't ignore the silly, obscured, deferred,
Lost soul's own goal, learning lessons
Away from home, Mummy's boy
Set loose on the world, curtailed,
Taken the best sure-fired test,
Lessons in life pushed to the limit,
Told I was the limit, pushy.
Drank Dad's elderflower wine,
The vault; easy distillery to thieve.
Took leave of my senses,
Drunken recompenses,
Climbing fences away from
Detention, barred in,
Considering bad behaviour,
Learnt how to disobey.
Controversy, my history,
Mum was too lenient.
Sad story, only boy,
Spoilt, difficult,
Charming, harming,
My way, first signs of disability.
Distorted, confused,
Nothing rang true,
Reject, effect,
Sisters had to,

Put up with the concept,
Bullish charm,
Attitude problem,
Bend rules,
To suit my turn.
Football my main concern,
Deflect, direct,
Past jumper post,
Empty space goal,
Loser consoled,
Victory paraded,
Avoid harassing,
Leading side deride,
Offside.
Decent decency,
Allows complicity,
Befriend friends,
Girl taken fishing,
No rod, sod off!
"Careful what you catch!"
Lad's jest,
All good fun at the rec.
What dialect,
Recounting talk,
Groups rebel,
Merry, hell, tell;
Heard it before,

Tell me more,
The one about?
Pulling leg yarn,
Joke, compare,
Dare, flare,
Have a go at,
Establishes sides,
Teams confide,
Surprising abides.
Stand, deliver,
Learn compromise,
Take, make,
Not a fake,
Original fraud,
Obscured, blurred,
Worried, heard
People say,
Got to one day,
America's right
To bear arms,
Put on a "T" shirt,
Bad attitude alludes,
No one to respect.
Challenge intellect,
Don't make do,
Put up with
Wrong all along.

Change, rearrange,
Not too late to,
Navigate a new course,
Of course, perverse,
Transverse route,
Root and branch,
Tree to a "T",
Climbing higher,
Not letting disability
Restrict me.
Keep doing
What I should,
If I could,
Swim off the pud,
Keep fit transpires,
Wear a nose clip,
To counteract the chlorine,
Shower well after,
Communal exercise the prize,
Wear goggles,
Be kind, good state of mind.
Sink or swim,
Play trim,
Count lengths,
More next time.
Combine, refine,
Practice turning,

Yearning confidence,
No pretence.
Exude doing,
Always been happy
To swim like a fish,
Something in my soul,
Or origin sea evolved,
Seal rolled,
Whale of a time,
Kelp yelp,
Slippy dippy,
Fun happy,
Short shorts,
Swim lengths,
At length.
Keep arm's length,
Long and short,
Fair retort,
Oblige deny.
Common decency,
Surprise myself,
Good behaviour,
Drilled instilled,
Came from home,
Parents taught,
Thought ignored,
Rebuffed enough,

Contrary country,
Contrary to beliefs,
Misspent argument,
Sloppy, diligent,
Once frequent,
Sake of argument,
Flaky disarray,
Hearsay says,
Commonplace,
Have disgrace.
Ashamed, blame,
Country mile,
Defile, trial,
No reason,
Tried pleasing,
Turned away,
From convalescence,
No better or worse.
Converse perturbed,
From peace of mind,
Want to be kind,
Smacked behind,
Left behind.
Leaders capitulate,
Seen it coming,
Good drumming,
Pitiful, unassailable.

Cheap sale,
Everything must go,
Above, below,
Asking price,
Cash in hand,
Drives a fair bargain,
Not reprimand,
Toe the line,
Keep in touch,
Stay connected,
Directly directed,
Affected affective.
Convert conversion,
My assertion,
Insist, persists,
Making lists.
Order of play,
Forget controversy,
Acceptable, delectable,
Beholder's beauty,
Bountiful desire,
Complicit, entire,
Completely admired,
Inspired trier,
Complier mire,
Get together, driver,
Had enough time,

To combine
A concubine,
Of seasoned fare.
Delicious dare,
Compare, rare,
Well-done run,
Bravo, escapist.

FORTUNATE LUCK

I like it when things click into place,
Plucky, lucky, ducky, clean mucky face,
Embrace good fortune, accept,
Detect goodwill when presented,
Take and make the best possible use of,
Good chance, correct stance, balance,
Stabilise, surmise true can-do,
Improper won't do,
Surely true,
Wrong stands out,
Must be corrected,
Directed henceforth,
For what it's worth,
Everything conserved,
Save and prosper,
Build and yield,
Profit taken,
Share what makes,
Not mistakes,
Fair compare,
Taken risks,
Now bliss.

INTO THE FRAY

Headlong into battle, taking on the wrong,
Got to be strong, not pushed around.
Starts with standing your ground,
Profound, look all around,
Different sides deride, comply,
Who's to say wrong from right?
Morals can get contrite.
Stay bright, alert, assertive,
Positive, sensitive, not dogmatic,
Initiative-taking directive, corrective,
Want to be elected friends on my side,
Got to be fair to both sides.
Correcting, assimilating, proving,
Get in the grove, diverge,
Purge, eliminate traits,
Know your own weakness,
Go from strength to strength.
Independent, bent, frequent,
Ask, challenge tasks,
Into the breach once more,
Shake, rattle and roll,
Console lost losers.

ADDICTION COMPULSIVE REPETITION

Before I was diagnosed with multiple sclerosis,
I knew something was wrong and was driven careless,
Started boozing, smoking marihuana to ease leg spasms, now a
proven therapy for MS.
Alcohol drowned my fears, hidden tears,
I was sobbing all alone, stoned, condoned,
Reckless on my motorbike, suicidal madness,
Tried taking heroin, too good, pretentious,
Doctors knew what was wrong,
Weren't inclined to say, as there was no treatment,
Said drinking would make it worse, perverse,
Smoking cannabis helped, habitual, out of it,
Grew my own, resourceful when needed,
Was aware it was sending spare gave up,
Only ate some, as medication drove me mad.
Psychotherapist set me straight down,
To me to regulate capitulate Neurologist,
Says how to deal with unbelievable deal,
Get real, accep,t adapt, contract, ascertain
My limits. Psychologist asks do I really,
Want to feel like this? Confess, skip duress,
Own up, have faith in naturally feeling good.
I have taken strides to do what I've got to do,

Because I want to be free from calamity,
Have aims, retain pride, not taken for a ride,
I confide, don't condone those who won't
Leave alone, expect too much from such,
Given up being dependent on dependants,
Relents, accept, augment arguments,
From bigots' diehard farts, fat lards, bastards,
Compulsions, urges, purges, manifestations,
Poor relations, confiscations taken away diligently,
Comparison adding contrast to going without,
Strong self-will, avoiding spills, assertive, directive,
Confidence, non-reliance on a buoyed-up sink,
Or swim a paradigm pattern to evolve, resolve,
Make it happen, transpire anyway, hearsay,
Congratulatory sycophantic brown-nose,
Creep complete defeat absolute defeated,
Completed hard-nosed supposed repose,
Convivial, detrimental to being mental,
Harassed supplemental, an addition
To being hustled, hassled,
Wheeler-dealer dispeller of what's needed.

SEASONS SEASONING

Go with the weather, sun cream on,
Base tan covering white all over,
Tanning brown, not pink, what do you think?
Sitting in the sun full on, shade breaks the parade,
Nicely displayed, insist ices left to devices,
Courtesy pleasingly, pleasantly, presenting itself,
Ice cream in a cone, flake traits permeate desire,
Dripping keeping the leading edge in play,
Turning around, tongues surround,
Chocolate flake engulfed all around safe and sound,
Dribble brings on quibble, look quick.
Image tarnished, fashion vanquished,
Put down across town, not popular
Anymore, always heading for a fall.
Different this season due to rhyme and reason,
Left behind, correct procedure averted,
Now reverted to old ways on displays,
Always the best consistently manifests,
With old androgynous boyish charm,
Disproves girls have the upper hand,
With command at Christmas time,
Presents of mind at season's season.

IDEAS AT NIGHT

Tablets taken at night, for my MS gives me insomnia,
I wake bolt upright at four in the morning,
Then I'm left to daydream and fantasise before I rise,
They can be deluded, alluded, often protruded.
I have a vivid imagination anyway;
This, compounded with sleepless thoughts,
Makes me unable to tell the difference between
Dreams, reality, imagined fictional happenings,
All mixed up together, not too clever,
Deliver a shiver at the thought of being a cosmonaut,
Lost in space, losing face, embarrassed at
Laughable, deluded concoctions,
Cocktails shaken, not stirred,
Dizzy, blurred, deferred words slurred,
Frustrated swearing as a trooper would,
Doing no good, misunderstood,
Sleep's haphazard,
Inventory invents obscurity; if believed, deceived.
Random collection, lost direction, affliction,
Harbouring duality, reality, calamity,
Perverse converse with the Devil takes me
On travels not suitable or sustainable,
Can't contain throwing life down the drain,
Persistent troubadour, wake! Deplore no more.

STAYING YOUTHFUL

Good state of mind to befriend,
Went swimming at seven o'clock this morning,
Got into the rhythm, kept going,
Sixteen lengths – somebody stop me!
Friendly, social activity, feelgood factor,
The chlorine has cleared all passages,
Sneezing, streaming, believing.
Try and swim more next time,
Good for mind, body, and soul,
Keeping fit a prerequisite to a youthful
State of mind, be kind to yourself and
Others, not abrupt, harsh; I feel lenient,
Younger scaremonger no longer,
Exuding, radiating happiness, no clash,
Panache didn't know I had, not bad,
Juvenile delinquent now frequents
At my own expense, how rich –
No expense spared, nice, no sacrifice,
Friendly, generous to share, not compare,
Young at heart, together an art, not apart.

OBVIOUS SAID

Repeating formatting,
I begin again, make it plain,
Want to sustain, input, divulge
What's been said before,
But in a more positive vein.
So, I must say it again plainly,
Spelling it out that counts for nowt,
Zip, nothing – thoughtless, senseless,
Repetitive rhyming slang reoccurring
Again and again, same old frame,
Get the picture? Depicted afflicted,
Taking it out on repetition itself,
Doing the same to retain solace,
Doesn't gain any respect, servitude,
Detected concurrence reflected, expected
From an imbecilic juvenile delinquent.
Immature, insecure, deplore – what for?
Enough said, the mighty dread common decency,
Has said it all before, behaving don't rave,
Or masquerade pretentious actor part.

OF COURSE, I WILL

You only must ask to take on that task,
My coarse humour does not demur,
The rough and smooth disproves,
Taking my time to remind, combine,
Harvest time – gather in the bushel,
Plenty to go around, grown from the ground,
Church organ plays hymn sounds,
All creatures, great and small,
Singing loudly, want to share
And spread around the community,
A generous opportunity to involve
Everyone dissolved, let down,
Having to pick up the left-over crop,
Wheat ears commandeer straw poll,
Those annulled from gathering in, surviving,
Thanksgiving shared by all stops the fall,
Not letting hunger take hold, resolve,
A problem shared, solved, good as gold,
Manifest bold, all told,
Of course, I will
Disparaging for the kill, coarsely won't do.

SOMETIMES NOT ALWAYS

I feel dreamy, sleepy, not alert,
Following the routine set straight,
Starts me off, delegate,
Lots on my plate, delete the trivial,
Want to be more convivial,
Check the usual drivel,
People's lives are non-sensical,
Find order in the same boring game,
Plain frame, not fanciful,
Housework tidied up,
My life a coffee cup.
Need purpose to surface,
Conformity curtains not drawn,
Wide sweeping view of the lawn dew,
The sun will burn back for you,
Hapless, I confess a stew,
Comradery needed,
Means to accept help,
Open to different way,
Wordplay crossword,
Devious knowledge,
Absurd reverb,
My lot is all I got,

Easy to forget,
Make the most
Of burnt toast,
Alarm, no harm,
Reset, air-clear,
A carbon slice,
Jam counteract,
Crunchy destruct,
Dialect plucked,
Shameless connect,
Try hard to remember
Life's purpose resembles,
Satisfaction, correct direction,
Away from defection,
Noisy suburbs reverb,
Navigate hate, displace
Violence, pretence,
Writing on the wall
Says it all and more,
Distraught extrovert,
Spray can reject,
Frustration expects,
More deplore what for,
Candid candour,
Quite frankly,
Expect direct,
Misplaced effect,

Assumes too much
From the ordinary,
Contrary, not satisfactory,
Displays conciliatory,
Peace-making revoking,
Laws to suit my own ways,
In a cloudy haze of
Promiscuity, nude
Magazine pictures,
Explicit poses of
Pornographic,
Explicit, elicit,
Shameful contraband,
Perverts demand
Silly used girls,
No pride derided,
The obscene exposed,
Lewd protruded,
Appetite misconstrued.
Food for thought,
Shouldn't be bought,
Refrain from blame,
Bold resolve,
Occupy my mind,
Positive thoughts,
How to move forward,
Acceptable, renewable,

Energy not costing the earth,
Must be the most positive
Adventure for a venturer
With handsome demure,
Being straightforward,
Straight, relate, contemplate,
All options considered,
Delete bad fate,
Not appreciated or related,
Confiscated unhealthy habits,
Not usual or accepted,
Behave, rave,
Think of others,
Sister, brother,
All the same, no other,
Love to accept direct
Forms of appraisal,
Like confirmations,
Friends yearn
On all terms,
Part of the party,
Not taking sides,
Talking to everybody,
Enhances my commodity,
Now included,
Ditch the deluded,
Game confused,

Clearer outside,
Agoraphobia deride,
Have pride
In everyday doing,
Life's pursuing,
Get it right,
Sometimes not always,
Held up by delays.
Patience is a virtue,
My impatience can't stand
Being a patient patient,
"Drop dead," I hear in my head,
Self-conscience said,
"Commandeer no fear,"
Fresh air, seeing stars,
Dizzy – sit down,
Collect my thoughts,
Not has been,
Done a lot,
Thankful for what I got,
Put on the spot,
Bail out with
Satirical humour,
Making fun
Out of life's conundrum,
All's said and done,
Repetitive, say again,

Moan, complain,
Put down,
Not fair, compare,
Level out,
Friends again,
All is not lost.

DON'T TOUCH IT

I've a sore spot and I can't help scratching,
Have been told a number of times to "leave it alone"!
I don't condone Matrons' reprimand; I must behave,
Or be in grave bad books, scornful bad looks,
For my own sake, don't be a flake annoyance,
Compliance – don't defy strict order, no OCD pleasure
In self-inflicted pain making the sore spot sorer,
Matron takes a hard line, no doubt defines,
For the best, no contest, manifest deluded,
Delusion's a pest, infests my mind, reminded
To not be blinded by persistent persistence,
Habitual habits inhabit, cohabit, deceptive,
Forceful, compulsive collateral, literal
Destructive manifestation, bad compilation,
Harming, deforming what should be left alone.

STRATEGIC LOGISTIC

Planning jobs to get them finished on time,
Shuffling a pack of cards, then dealing
From the left, several hands, fair play,
Look at what I've got to sort indiscriminately,
So as not to reveal my lot, got a plot,
Individual cards played randomly,
Keeping my cards close, no ruse,
Confidently confuse the strategy,
Look like a card sharp,
Deal and shuffle, no tomorrow,
Poker face giving nothing away.
Shuffle, no reason to my strategy,
Logically ruthless card play,
Commandeering is subject to flattery,
Strategic endorsed competitiveness,
Playing out, counting cards gives
The upper hand to my command,
Dare to be fair, compare cards held,
Knowing what must be left face down,
Hoping for a floater — ace, jack, change suit,
Organising my strategy to foil all comers.

WHAT'S NOT TO LIKE

Plenty, particularly this saying,
Obnoxious, agreeable summary
That I'm supposed to agree with,
Obviously, go along or be square,
Put on the spot, no choice of opinion,
Had my mind made up for me,
The projector knowing better,
Get with it, complicit, illicit,
Standard set manifest, correct,
Direct effect, aesthetic assumed,
Beautiful plume all aplomb,
Magic done, continuum more,
Don't know what for applauded,
Happy to ignore, seen before,
Directed applause censored,
Edited, suppressed opinion,
Not my dominion, party,
Hearty comparison elected,
Now defected comparison,
Contrast too broad, wide, defied,
Harassed won't confide,
Tried denied opinion not mine.

LIFE'S EXPERIENCE

Gives me confidence to live,
Doing things automatically,
Just second nature, done before,
Sometimes doing what came before.
How did I know what to do?
It was in my bones' DNA,
I must have inherited the concept,
Applied to my dialect, "can do".
A natural who knows,
Uncanny understanding,
Straight ahead, not reprimanding,
Easy as a knife cutting butter.
Never played golf before,
Holed good with the putter,
Got the concept from watching,
Easy to know what's next.
Don't look perplexed,
Gifted, God only knows,
Got the tune composed,
Standards set, diagnosed,
Contrived, written down,
Sensible experience sells.

ANTICIPATING BETTER

Always hopeful for things to go my way,
Many things could improve,
Disabled having to make do,
Simple things are difficult,
Needing help to get dressed,
Finding clean clothes from the drawer,
My foot seems a long way away
From being able to adorn socks,
Can't reach with legs crossed,
Prominent toes catch famously,
Annoyingly, hideously, frustratingly,
"Yelp" doesn't help feign pain, try again,
Persistence is my resistance to failure,
Stubborn family asset appreciated,
Bringing back memories of tantrums –
Ice cream solves the resolve,
Grew up as a pain in the butt,
My way controversy get want,
Determined urchin evolving,
Know how to get regret winning,
Embarrassed over trying for better.

EVERYONE'S FRIENDS

I would like to think so,
We have learnt to live together,
Whatever the weather,
Personal beliefs, religion,
Different sides of the fence,
Culture can point out differences,
How to think on the blink,
Reassured, confide pride,
Taken for a ride, speak out,
Spoken for, married,
Respect parried,
Forgiveness harried,
Weight carried,
Platonic friends' amends,
Get it straight, delegate,
A job well done paid for,
Trusted reputation,
Carry the can person,
Always an Art,
On the right side proliferate
To making friends,
Give and take, perpetuate.

DRAW A LINE IN THE SAND

The limit of my ambition,
That's to say no further,
Got my limits, that's the limit,
He's the limit, no end to
Save all boundaries,
Hit for six over the top,
Border clear-cut,
Which side are you on?
If I stand here, you'll be over there,
Faraway eyes criticise,
Near but distant,
Resistant to all,
Shrug off calls,
Former barrier
Up, let in,
Embrace people,
Embarrassed, self-conscious,
Bold over the threshold,
Now sold on told,
Part of party,
Not left out,
Line sublime,
Over and above,

Thought of restriction,
Different dialect,
Accept, defend,
Comprehend, amend,
Best of friends,
Hope to see you again,
Friendlier, defer,
Not too strong,
Gently Bentley,
Frequently asked,
Different contrast
To last time.
Ironic humour,
Makes fun of
The same routine,
Done again against
All odds, sod off,
Leave me alone,
Don't condone,
What's obviously
My style of impressing,
Not cross-dressing,
Wearing shorts in the rain,
Flash in the pants,
Show-off actor,
Enjoying the reaction,
Jealous disdain,

Not in the main picture,
The green-eyed monster,
Foreign juxtaposition,
Composition unusual,
Deferred protraction,
Same reaction,
Expected contraction,
Gullible take
On harbingers,
Well-endorsed rich,
Posh show-offs,
Toffs, braggarts,
Haggard looks,
Old age has endorsed
Weathered wrinkles,
Sun-tanned characterful man
Looking disdainfully distinct,
A handsome Italian Traveller
Gentleman of the road
Who won't be told
Which way to go,
A look of disbelief,
About-turn confirms,
He's stubborn, lonely,
What-for poor,
Seen it all before,
A precious deplore

No more than is
Usually usual,
Can't take anymore,
Need shelter from
The next storm, forlorn,
Get under cover,
Bless-the-weather,
Hell-for-leather,
Gathered, harnessed,
Whatever you discover,
The line has been crossed,
Tide's coming in anyway,
Castles dismissed,
Flags withdrawn with scorn.

REBEL WITHOUT A CAUSE

Started by wanting to be different,
An individual forging my identity,
Started smoking to look hard,
Got a moped driven mad,
Drank pints down the pub,
Image was everything,
Jeans, denim jacket, cost a packet,
Music broad with it heavy and soft,
Art, trendy style copied,
Tried out all, borrowed, stole,
Cajoled girlfriends, made amends,
Worked to spend around the bend,
Friends helped, talked, rebuked,
Set straight, changed my mind, kind,
Reprimanded, demanded, landed,
More fool me, you to do blue,
Get the latest melody maker,
Pretend faker perchance immediately,
Romance, no chance, set balance,
Second hand will do, ask you,
Compatriots oblige my turn,
The latest trends go with it, complicit,
Change for the better to the letter,

Fierce competitor, detractor,
Max-Factor label sells sold,
Monopoly played, laid out,
Leaving no doubt influence,
Capitalist in the making,
Must do better, improve,
Rise to the occasion, expand,
Lift conversationalists, persist,
Talk until rebelled again,
From picture frame, blame,
Can't contain or regain
What's lost at a cost,
No repost done diddled,
Fiddled my way, controversy,
Fair play is what I say,
Seem to have found my way,
Taken a chance, compounded
Ideas looking forward to
Assertive directive giving me a cause
To be proud of not recklessly confessing,
Or, under duress, the jury says "keep the peace",
Or face the consequences nonetheless.

PHLEGM

Must be dispelled from your mouth,
Depending on the viscosity,
Will determine how far you can gob,
If it's a bit frothy, bubbly, not far,
Most of it on your sleeve,
Strands attached around your face.
Full disgrace if you can't gob
Out clearly, no density,
A good spit is spat with venom,
Clearly clearing obstructions
With attitude, protrude, conclude,
The dispelled not held out,
Rolled around the mouth,
To form a protrusion, delusion,
A lump perfectly formed
With weight, not to castigate,
Delegated to lower regions,
Out and away, impressive display,
Good delivery commonplace,
No disgrace, lose face,
Spat race.

DREAM TOO MUCH

All part of living is having ideas,
Projecting oneself onto a scene,
I do wake up thinking, "Got to write that down",
Before it's lost, forgotten,
Many are vivid, overactive,
Sometimes haunted by said,
Getting me out of bed,
Disturbed mind, be kind,
Stuck in my head, can't
Get rid of stubborn lingering,
Distracted by all-day memories,
Abstracted thoughts,
Pulled apart art,
Expressionist concept,
Making an impression,
Cut-and-paste haste,
Metre, rhythm, and rhyme,
Collected collage,
Paper on the board,
Gone like a dream,
Composition balanced
Revealing extremes.

OH, MY NATURE

First light, sunny, clear, bright,
Got to be right on everyone,
Slow down, take it all in,
Stop masquerading, get real,
The feeling is beautiful, absorb it,
The air is thin, gasping,
The sun will burn through,
Cream on my arm to stop harm,
Clouds floating, offering no protection,
Cover up a fair complexion
Is the right direction,
Aware of the connection,
Rouge, bare, compare,
Tan well, dispel,
As far as I can tell,
Got me under its spell,
Can't stay under too long,
Burning ambition, confession,
Doting small doses
Is enough bluff D stuff,
Duff burn confirm,
Areas not covered,
Discovered by a lover,

The rosy hue,

Humming a tune,

Carefree bloom,

Tree pollen sullen,

Sneezes appease,

Honey counteracts,

Favourable effect,

Hayfever,

Streaming eyes,

Comprise, defy,

Suck a lemon,

Sweet honey,

Nose runny,

Throat sore,

Over act bore,

Poor commentary,

Sent to Coventry,

Say no more,

Take coarse,

Rough and smooth,

Make the interlude protrude.

Stick it out and pout.

IRONY

Can be funny, good humour to get,
Some people who are too serious don't,
Matter-of-fact, direct, sensible,
Stupid to joke about, turnabout,
An unusual way of saying trouble
At the double, could be worse,
Converse, light take on fake,
Doesn't always make for rapport,
Talking sense, no recompense,
For derogatory mickey-taking,
Humorous analogy, loose talk,
Similar to recall, I recall all for
Not wanting to upset the balance
Of good manners, appreciating the latter,
For better or worse, converse,
Could be worse, rehearsed blame,
Over again, apology for a reason,
Set to repeat, delete, or return to
Lost ways, drunken haze, ironically
Pondering diverse ways to say,
I'll do it again differently but the same.

DOUR

Feeling down, a bit low,
Looking depressed,
Having trouble rising above,
An air of repression,
Brought down, renowned for,
Characteristic of a distinguishing
Feature ascertained,
Belonging to my personality,
Something to put up with,
Part of the performance,
Having a way with words,
Low-tone speech,
Successful streaks,
Assertive confidence,
Unreproachable stance,
Character eloquence,
Doesn't make sense,
Sitting on the fence,
Contravening rules
For unintelligent fools,
Consolation drooled,
Unrepentant abuse,
The trait relates to haste,

Quickly, now waste,
Bothered by disdain,
Pickup, regain,
Don't allow it to drain,
Conformity confirming
To the allotted procedure,
Tedious, repetitious,
Unnegotiable calamity,
About to set
Jam in a jam,
Pan boiled,
Bubbled over
The rim, asking,
Not setting,
Lemon rind,
Pectin assures,
Ripple devours,
Spread on bread,
Confectionary said,
Lifting not dour
Anymore,
Candour applause.

FICKLE

You can't do everything yourself,
I must tactfully ask people for help,
Usually, they are willing to comply,
As I am in a wheelchair, to be fair,
I must be patient and fit in,
Everybody is busy; just a second,
Often wait at the gate, delegate,
Can't castigate, wait in turn,
Organising other people
Is a skill in itself.
Asking tactfully to humour
Breaks the ice, makes fun
Of my humbleness,
My situation of helplessness.
I haven't always needed help,
Now I beg, borrow, steal, deal,
Not a sycophant, grateful,
Try my best to contest,
Contest problems as seen,
Meet head-on, solve, resolve,
Positive, not fickle, show metal.

SAILING FAST

Very windy sailing day,
Surf blowing off the top,
Waves breaking in streaks,
Lines left trailing white,
Deep blue-green turquoise,
Noise silent, then blast,
Feeling bullish, give it a go,
Worst to happen? Swim;
Able, done before,
Crew team with Miss Pinafore,
Kitted out in a dry suit
With oils, spoils,
Take on a blast,
Brave, not last,
Contrast blue,
Want to do,
Moody true,
Prove I can do,
Demonstrate,
Watcher's rue,
Think next time,
Breathless gasps,
Surge past,

Get hold of,
Boat plane,
Take off,
Wake behind,
Stream left,
To remind,
Trail hind,
Pick up on a wave,
Surf down,
Into the next rising,
Into, through,
In control, out of control,
Adrenalin lifts,
Surge forward,
Gaining ground
On the trailblazer,
Setting course,
Overtake,
Leave behind,
"Water, please!"
Around the mark,
Disembark a lark,
Wind whistles,
Beaufort scales,
Up a level,
Serious drivel,
Great laugh,

At speed,
More plead,
Satisfies need,
Concede greed,
Full of speed,
Exact aspect,
Achieved goal,
Cheer one-up,
Faster, faster,
Correlation addiction,
Don't slow down,
Want more,
Got used to fast,
Now usual,
Customary customer,
Accustomed to
This formality,
Impressive regularity,
Assured applaud,
Carry on carrying out,
Conducting from the stand,
Orchestra at my command,
Play a sea shanty,
Popeye the sailor man
Carries the can,
Back around, head for shore,
Dryland, make a stand,

Tie the boat down.
Stop the rush,
Addictive speed,
Satisfied need,
Stillness concede,
Finished race,
Know my place.

LEARN TO LIVE AGAIN

Blank face – what do I stand for?
Not sure about anything,
I'm breathing, still alive,
Routine followed, borrowed idea
From a song ear-wormed in my head,
Not paying royalties, just stuck,
Same-old, same-old growing old,
Success of the song, diddle-dum,
Life's conundrum at work, shirk,
Aware of repeating, deleting,
Start anew again, ascertain
What's been done before.
More, deplore at core, all for,
Don't expect a magic change,
Novel ways of writing subjective,
To personal subjects subjectively,
In order to form a new order,
Bringing on a different tune,
Neurotic rhyme sublime,
Wishful thinking, sinking
Into old ways, disobey,
New ideology, rescue pathology,
Way of thinking to maintain,

Regain interest in the subject matter,
That does matter, matter of fact,
Boring, no tact; should know better,
Considering where I've been and
What I've done, still want to learn
More, new interests digest into,
Alternative views ways of looking
At old subjects with an atmosphere,
Of change its juxtaposition into,
Different setting next to disproportionate,
Disparity of conglomerates disparity,
Needing to change, rearrange plainly,
As a mark of respect, learning to deflect,
All subsidiary supplementary benefits,
To give a complementary, beneficial
Benefit to all concerned with an
Appraisal that praises with "no".
Apparition apparently deceiving,
Fragmentary, disconnected, rudimentary
Conceptions of living life to the full; no bull.

FOR SURE

A saying, word of mouth,
Dogmatic figure of speech,
Positive expression,
Complementing, admire,
Supplementing desire,
Complement adoration,
Getting the balance right,
"That's right!"
Analogy the same,
Attractive comment,
Repent again,
Sustain blame.
Many meanings
Definitely will
Oblige compromise.
Do it again,
Won't abstain,
Complaint retained,
Give up, retire,
Set on fire,
Going good, going well,
Slap on the back.

SIMPLE THINGS PLEASE

Boring appeasing the in-the-know,
I've mollified the prerequisite details,
Certified plans, acknowledged them,
Sent back duplicate copies,
The so desired had expired, tired,
A formal appraisal convivially done,
A set process complied by, not denied.
Adhered to procedure by return,
Wheels in motion, turning around,
Getting the job off the ground,
Not letting problems compound,
Confidence asserted, confirmed,
It had all been agreed before
A statute declared by law,
Making the whole job a bore,
Taking time, costing more,
The simplest procedure can't ignore,
Done in a trice, genuinely nice,
Complicit procedure complied with,
Nothing denied, pan-fried,
Contrive the expected, directed,
Effective, oblige, connive, done.

WHITER THAN WHITE

Means covering up misdemeanours,
Wrongs done, wanting to correct,
Bit suspect, bending rules to suit,
No fooling, deluding senses recompense,
Naive, thought you'd get away with it,
Embarrassed, caught out; stop, thief!
Corruption coverup made good,
Understood, lenient, wayward,
Make good if you could,
Try to negotiate but a bit late,
Back peddling, confiscate,
Face head-on to terminate,
Problem sorted, aborted,
Clouds clearly see clear,
Clarity unmuddied, fud-e-dudied,
Old ways dismayed delays today,
Have to say obliterate the considerate,
White, see-through, defy, darkly hidden,
Disembark, set off,
Half-truths aloof,
Bad, hit the roof,
Lost truths – white lies compromise.

OFFERED HOPE

By reading about new developments with MS,
New treatments seemed obvious and proven,
Using one's own stem cells from DNA in the blood,
Can be enhanced, selected, developed then,
Given back to the donor, enriching bodies,
Potential to repair damage previously done,
Myelin that is scarred and dysfunctional can
Be repaired and restored back to fully functional,
Operational use, walking, moving, looking around,
Normal, safe and sound, profound improvement,
From previous disability – a calamity to me!
Learnt to appreciate what I can do, trying hard to
Get back to as normal a life as possible.
Difficult when you're impatient, frustrated, and
Expect more from yourself, limitations dwell,
As a spell of misfortune, unfortunate regret.
I am connected to websites offering help,
As there are many more like me, disabled,
Needing information and to talk to each other,
A problem shared is a problem solved, I'm told.

THINKING ALOUD

It does help to speak what I've written,
Mind's eye applied, put down as said,
Literary mistakes over-ruled
As a matter of making sense,
Not just to me but everyone.
Talking to yourself isn't madness,
Just confidence in being right,
Trying out its sounds,
Before writing it down;
Reality in guises
Surely reaffirm,
Manners maketh man,
Old is bold, I'm told.
Speaking out upfront,
Clearly, dearly,
Got it sincerely.
Thinking proud,
Allowed to pronounce,
Correctly defect,
Change course,
Reality changes,
Subtly rearranges.

DRIVING SPARE NOT FAIR

Irritations irritate my usual navigation;
Want to start on the right foot,
Get away from important sway,
Clear conscience delivered,
Exude good mood.
Annoyances trivial,
Time wasters abandoned,
Small minds left behind,
Usual routine combined.
Making, contemplating
Putting together from a list,
Connecting bassist,
Parts assembled
To resemble structure,
Of a larger-than-life
Person, a caricature.
Cartoon characters
Resembling those seen
On television,
Out of context,
Different mood,
Colours rude.

POWER OF SMELL

Instantly brings back visual memories,
Of where I was, what I was doing, and when.
Could be back in childhood, adolescence,
The canvas of an old tent put up in the rain,
Family fighting over where to sleep – complain.
Now the sound of a mallet hammering in pegs,
Throwing out dregs, filling water cans,
Kettle on – a cuppa makes amends,
Friends again, sorry, borrow,
Get ready to do it tomorrow.
Leaders follow instincts smelt,
Catapult wars, argument deplores,
My side is better than yours?
Competition, no pleasing, barracking.
Feel better for convalescing,
Taking time on my holiday
To unwind from work pressures,
Imposed, supposed, suppressed
Countless times, immeasurable,
Have burnt, learnt not to seal lose,
Control of frayed ends loose ends,
Best smelt smoke carries parried.

WORTH THEIR SALT

Salt has always been a valued commodity;
It preserves food to be stored,
Sodium chloride – a clear powder
Sprinkled on meat stops the rot,
Preserves reserves held in reserve,
Fish kept fresh from the salty,
As if just caught from the briny
Timely, this big, assuredly,
Definite affinity,
A positively big gain worthy of remaining,
Contained in cellar salt cellar,
Retrieved from the sea by evaporation.
Salt crystals left to be stored away
For use another day, historical commodity,
Comes into play another day, saves the day,
Preserves time, frozen to be unwoven.
Priceless value assessed worth contained,
Regained additive to resolve a new taste,
Delicious flavours enhanced, entranced,
Balance sets stall for added to the preserve.

GOOD AND READY

Suggestive somebody stop me!
Going boldly henceforth,
Taking on anything in my way,
Confidently, courteously, bravely.
Not going to let trivia deflect me
From standing proud, loud, and clear,
Chivalrous champion, charming,
Well-mannered, good-humoured.
Exuding self-righteous deliverance,
Expectance, non-reoccurrence of
Overzealous manic forth righteous,
Consolidation accumulating,
Pending arbitration to decide who takes on
The very next decisive pervade of,
Skiving out in disorderly fashion,
Making a mockery of true travesty,
Belittling, putting down what was
Once mine, held high above
What was seen as fair rapport,
Offering candour, candid
Singularity, exponentially
Growing to a larger-than-life
Character with deceptive charm,

Making allowances for stuttering,
Bashful, embarrassed by his
Charming, effeminate delivery,
Causing rapturous, raucous
Laughter due to pernicious,
Insidious differentials of opinion,
With no dominion plain to see.
Friendly comradery, humour
Used as a safety valve to excuse,
Pretentious delivery breaking the
Ice with friendly advice on how to get
Around said legal problems forthwith,
Without any difficulties henceforth.
An allowance has been benefacted
Into the equation by my sponsor,
Patron patronising my humour,
Adding to my jokes with a poke
At my aroused jiggery-pokery,
With the slickness of a politician about
To be unseated, a right candidate,
As of late, indeterminate delegate.

THROW CAUTION TO THE WIND

Nevertheless, being careful not to upset,
Whatever you do, there seems to be consequences,
Liabilities involving set laws, litigation,
Requiring arbitration to keep the peace,
I just want to be free,
To do what I want to do,
Even that is a commodity.
Walking along a lane footpath,
Must be careful not to stray
On anybody's property carelessly,
Dogs, cows, bulls protect, foreign
Dialect comes from down the road,
Mistaken identity, calamity, neighbours
Rue, can-do possession, dereliction of duty.
On your guard, befriend, try hard,
Conciliatory to everybody, affirmative,
Big softy, really – reality, abstractly
Detracts matter-of-factly, wooden delivery.
Not holding back, let go, lose your feet,
By the undertow forced to swim against
The current, powerful draw away from the beach,
Out of reach, can't stand, front crawl to land,
Saved myself, still alive, back to the beach,

Towel – quite a dish waiting for me,
Impressed by my swimming to safety,
Thought I would be pulled away.
Saved by dramatic strength at length,
Not widths, pit my wits against lost souls,
Vagabonds', drunkards', good friends,
Fun time, the paramount objective sets
Good timers' objective as standard,
Usual for debauched wicked youngsters,
One following the other, leading,
To go one better to the letter,
Upsetter of who can hold their beer,
Before throwing their weight about.
Aggression – a lesson to be learnt,
Losing their head, alcohol talking,
Bravado threatens, daring to go one
Better, downing more than ever before.
Just one more, then I'll stop; promise!
More damage done in the name of fun,
Foolhardy, false comradery bullied up,
Sick as a pup, in a mess, I confess,
My limit reached yet again, can't refrain,
Drunken bum crawling home all alone,
Don't condone my behaviour, leave me alone.
Dread the morning, sick as a dog,
Flogged sprog, basket case, down eyes;
No surprise after the amount I drunk,

Sympathy not given, humiliated,
Blame myself, left on a shelf, continue,
Never learn, affirm, directly spent,
Lost out on frequent frequently.
Asked questions about what to do,
My answer is, don't wait or hesitate,
Implicate, navigate around
The estuary sound full of buoys,
People playing with aqua toys,
Staying afloat on boats, sailing,
Tacking up, wind avoiding, grounding
On shallows marked by orange
Marker buoys, challenging channels,
Flowing swiftly past, aghast at the contrast
Of stiff breezes surging past, lifting
To higher horizons, archipelagos,
Beautiful origins, new beginnings,
Throwing caution to the wind.

LOUD AND CLEAR
OVER AND OUT

Plainly, simply, bluntly,
Roger, over and out,
Military sign signal,
Accepted acknowledgement,
Right oh, it will be done,
Sure-thing conundrum.
Right away, no delay,
Common decency,
Hearsays said,
Moral dread.
Confirm about-turn,
Heels click together,
Stand tall, proud,
Regiment augment,
No argument, relent,
Pent-up anger,
Harassment, consent,
Belligerent frequent,
Decent dissent from
All decency, conciliatory.

INQUIRY

I want to launch an inquiry into doing the right thing;
I was enquiring if this was appropriate,
At this stage of the proceedings.
I was taking things literally,
Perhaps too literally,
Conversing with conversationalists
Who had a particular, pedantic
Way of asserting their authority.
Talking light-heartedly, brightly,
With a sinister twist and turn,
Which I was soon going to learn
About enquiring into humour.
Taking it in the right way,
Not personally aimed at
Anyone or any group,
But used ridicule as
A pervasive inquiry
Into enquiring about –
Should this be a logical
Inquiry into disseminating,
Broadcasting views,
So that everybody who enquired.

CONSIDERATE BEHAVIOUR

Having to think about all options,
I want to avoid all discrepancies
And be consistent with my format,
Which is planet first, stop abusing,
Must understand the problem
Then take positive action.
Firstly, correct my standing,
Improve what's loose,
Tighten the obtuse,
Leave out abuse,
Not casual,
Serious, convivial.
Got to be liveable,
Serious, not trivial,
Making plans, amend
What's expected,
Anticipated,
Predicted the reply.
Converse rehearse,
Again and again,
Get things right,
Stop the blight.

NARRATIVE

My narrative is lyrical with meter,
A descriptive form of poetry
In an essay explanation,
Matter-of-fact enquiry,
Monologue story,
Psychology good,
Philosophy true,
Rhyme sublime,
Defined clearly.
Explanatory, regularity,
Thesaurus,
Definite definition,
Definitive conclusion,
Offering a solution,
Presenting, enquiring,
Resolve devolved,
Control censored.
Appreciation admired,
Sure-fired,
Efforts combined,
Conclude conclusion,
No delusion.

DISTRACT DEFLECT

Annoying thoughts bother me,
Much like an unwanted tune,
Obnoxious, opinionated, possessive
Cretins take control of my droll.
Sense of humour is devoid,
Stand tall, annoyed,
Precocious, moralistic, opinionated,
Try to block my advance.
Been here before, bore, deplore,
Try to endure with candour,
Take it on the chin,
Turn the other cheek.
Be meek, deplete,
Avoid trolled trollies,
Frustrated dollies,
Make it real, peel off
The charade of toff.
Better scoff,
Deluded, protruded,
Pernicious, pedantic,
Finickity, pluralistic,
With no harmony.

LYRICAL NARRATIVES

Self-deduction has made me realise
That my writing fits this genre,
It is a natural progression, the way of working for me,
It combines telling a story on a relevant subject
That I have in mind, needing to explore.
My style of writing poetic essays is inclusive,
My way of addressing said topic henceforth,
Enjoyable for me, hopefully the reader too,
I always try to write with humour to keep the interest
By being not too serious, jovial.
Definitely, when seriously funny,
A reward for being absurd –
Fun is a good state of mind,
Playful, being kind, remind,
The plot unravels to reveal
Fortuitus happenings happening,
Superfluous to the occasion,
Countless plots is what I got.
Assuredness is my lot, can't stop
An actors plot, final curtain,
Take my leave now, bow!

TALK TO PEOPLE

Yes, it's important to talk, make conversation,
So that you're not taken the wrong way;
Seen as ignorant, belligerent, blind,
Barriers are put up if not flexible,
There is a level of accepted decency
That must be overcome to pertain,
Remain in the picture doing the right thing,
Which is a moral obligation, confronting
Common difficulties presented to us all,
Not including personal beliefs or laws.
A way must be pertained to be listened to,
Combatting combat is essential to ridicule,
So is dismissively dismissed as futile,
Corresponding with correspondents can
Present the presence of mind to be kind,
Not let irregular regulations differ diffusely,
Causing the obtuse, obliquely, obstinately,
Obsessively, in the original format formatting,
Forging familiar familiarities frequently,
With my family talking my way out
Of being too familiar with friendships –
In my fraternity, friendly fellowships follow.

FOREVER YOUNG

Still got a boyish outlook,
As old as you feel, I'm sticking to it,
I wonder how old I look.
Difficult to assess age in others,
I lost my hair years ago,
Don't think my skin is wrinkly.
Not taking children, grandchildren to school,
Still play the fool, kick a ball,
Haven't retired, always self-employed.
Have a routine allotted by cups of tea,
Have usual habits; Friday fish and chips,
Don't drink, smoke, normal bloke.
Aroused by normality, children left home,
Do the usual, mostly formal,
Proud, loud, hide from the crowd.
Nothing too radical, enjoy clean fun,
Sit in the garden, play cards,
Take in the sun, charades.
Always a laugh at school, fool,
Can't grow out of that, play the prat,
Forever young, my son.

A CREEL

Fishing basket,
Collecting a catch,
Shiny colours,
Revealing dolours.
Small sprat, that,
Barely a meal,
Return to sea,
Larger quantity;
Family to feed,
Growing greed,
I concede wanting
More, their call.
Provide sufficiently –
Not enough
Is not good enough.
Foodstuffs
Stops gruff,
Attitudes disrupt,
Demands made
By fellow comrades.
Happiness parades,
Various charades.

FINDING ORDER

I appreciate, more than ever, a sense of order,
Things I've done in the past seem rushed,
Without consideration of their value.
Now going back, having to untangle a scramble
Of ideas jotted down around a theme,
Which has now grown into a promising subject,
Having grown into something groovy,
Developed and enlarged, improved upon,
From a small acorn, now a tree,
That I want to climb higher with a better,
Clearer view of what I've embarked upon.
Lyrical narrative is my style,
Now I have found the confidence to pursue
An important theme, now rolling along,
Identity found in my personality.
Priceless, growing into it with relish,
A commodity must do more, can't stop,
I now need an editor to make sense,
And collate into a proper, readable format,
From abstract dialect, singing, rhyming,
Keeping it together, bling borrowing
Into the right kind of thing, ding-a-ling.

TWISTING WORDS

Around so that they sound right,
In a format bright, not contrite,
Get them in a rhythm dancing,
So, they are enhancing each other,
Producing a line of defence,
Commenced with straight from the heart,
Emotional, take part, dart
From the obvious, devious,
Manufactured mischievous,
Fun to be had, glad, sad,
Taking the mickey out of,
Sounds rehearsed,
Common old verse,
Heard reverbed verbs,
Consulting absurd,
The ridiculous occurs,
Proverb enhanced,
Half a chance,
Taken, spoken for,
Beautiful, demure,
Candid score,
Put away controversy.

STEREOTYPES

Forced into a situation of complying with what's
Expected of me, how wrong they can be;
I'm not like that, I have values assuredly.
A dodgy deal made me feel unreal,
A bit cheap and nasty, plastic, fantastic,
My decision was not Jurassic, fossil-fuelled,
A relic from the past, contrast annulled.
Straighter than I realised, defensive,
Argumentative, to be fair, I'm as contrair as seen,
Belligerent, stubborn, derisive, congestive.
Fair play, unexpected controversy
Causing a calamity with disparaged,
Anomalous, unidentified personage
Of irregular vernacular, strange at first glance,
Dizzy, perchance, at the odd encumbrance.
A hindrance, lost the chance of resemblance,
Identity formed as an original commodity,
Resigned, left alone, only to condone
All superfluous, pretentious activities
That occur under duress, nonetheless.
With no purpose other than a right royal scam,
Done again and again; no one to blame.

OWN CHANCES

I must make my own chances,
Every man for himself,
Without being selfish, considerate,
I research options to take
What's possible and grips me.
It would be nice to, but no, done it before,
If I tackled it differently, new interest,
But no, I'm depressed.
An old song brought on a tear,
Bringing back happy memories
Of life being clear, lots of space,
My fall from grace displaced.
How to counteract with contacts,
Can't rely on others not to bail out,
Must try analysing satisfaction,
My reaction is complicated.
A simple answer isn't at hand,
Wrapped up in myself!
Won't let go of constraints,
Holding back what makes,
Solves, resolves, consoles,
A lost soul, rigmarole, foul play.

DIFFICULT PHYSICAL

I love making things but am now restricted,
This is why writing is now my favourite –
I construct a narrative poem to explain,
Piecing together, constructing a plot,
Build a lyrical formulation dictum
That describes my contradiction.
Unable to proceed, advance,
Putting together a series of analogies,
Likewise forming and building positively,
Brick by brick, a physical object constructed.
Lego comes to mind, clean, moribund,
A maquette example to build upon,
A sound idea singing clear in my ear,
With no fear of contravening the building
Regulations; now all's said and done.
Able, not a conundrum, challenging
Not disparaging, belittling grandiose ideas
In my head put forward architecturally,
In a drawing plan showing all elevations,
Plan the north-south side, vertical, horizontal,
That isn't detrimental to its vicinity incremental.

GET SUPPLIES

Stock up,
Refill, empty,
Gone quickly,
Run down,
Come down
To a moment
In time,
Shared with you.
Cherished,
Replenished,
Run out,
Take, make,
Give, share,
Only fair,
I care.
Emotional pair,
Basics cost,
Not lost,
In out,
All about
Necessary
Quantity,
Derisory,

Affinity,

Functionality,

Punctuation,

Correct, direct,

In effect,

More or less.

Decent dissent,

Disagree,

Replenish,

Commodity,

Give service –

Not lip service.

Kiss and make up,

Refuelled,

Harsh annulled,

Diverge,

Split up,

Continue up

Not down,

Bad state,

Delegate,

Assign, relate.

RUNNING LATE

Waiting for the salesman, should be here,
Water softener up the spout,
Sell or fix a bag of tricks,
In the mix, sort out,
"It's knackered mate!"
Loud and fast, given to me straight,
Barrage of leaflets and costs,
Bull-headed, fast conquest,
Best to go ahead, special
Deal revealed– no extra cost.
One left, pay later by card,
Hard bargain, same again,
Pertain, complain, remain,
Got the gist, list, persist.
Free fitting, not costing,
A host of other gains,
Take, always cancel
If not satisfied, deride.
Now complied, can't hide,
Proficient delivery,
Sold on liaison after terms.

HOT PURSUIT

Rush-chasing takers,
On the make, steal,
"Come back, stop, thief!"
Bounders' confounders,
At large, mirage
Of misplaced louts,
Taking the upper hand command,
I'm losing out, "Shout!"
That's mine,
Lambast sad cast.
Twist of fate accomplice,
Derisory thieves on their knees,
Don't please, laugh, tease,
Joke's on me, discrepancy.
Not going to let them get away,
Decency tells me to retrieve reason, thieving,
Got the number of the getaway car,
They're not going far, a little dysentery,
Causing calamity for yours truly.
Call the police, they track the tracks,
Bounders now on the rack,
Fighting back, hot rod crashes.

COPING WITH MADNESS

Most of the time, I feel fine,
But it's not long before distortion sets in,
Depending on how I've slept;
If well, good order and happiness resides,
Peace of mind – a good state to be in.
Overpowering bad thoughts can take over,
So, I must not let them question their assertion,
They will take over, become believable, if allowed,
I must ask myself, will this really happen?
Deal with problems as they occur,
Clear away derogatory, depressing hearsay
That has happened, overactive imagination,
The conclusion is careful assessment.
As I go, be fair, don't dare, tread carefully,
Tactfully, assuredly, safely, confidently,
Easy-peasy, get in the groove,
Channel true thoughts correctly.
Most people are straight, delegate
Difficult jobs, harassment will linger,
Keep cool, don't be a fool to yourself,
Sod money, wealth, stealth,
Keep your mind in good health.

MAKING SPACE

At the right pace to embrace,
Next problem, attention needed,
Coping with life's daily routine.
Set out a task to unmask hindrances,
What's holding me back, finding the knack,
I know what to do, just have to do it.
Making a start is the art, take part,
Have checked all the trivial convivial,
Act out, stretch, protraction, spin.
Realising I've changed my ways,
Has left an uncertain future ahead,
Exciting, what might be.
Should be deliberately definite,
Clear all trackers pinching ideas,
Want to move forward with them;
Made space for them to exist,
Started, struck off the list, persist.
Insisted on conquering conquest,
If only to ditch the phoney baloney,
Need help but realise it's down to me.
Almost catastrophic if I don't make space
For creative expression, direction, impressions.

FAMILY GATHERING

Great to see everyone after the Covid lockdown,
Hugs, kisses at a respectable distance,
Young welcomed into the fold,
New bonding between, all fun, laughter all round,
Safe and sound as a pound, inflation deferred,
Food barbequed, fizz splashed out, good sparkle.
Tales of hardship told, friendship bold,
Young and old console young tears, dears,
Much talk between years counteract fears,
Troubles agreed upon, stupidity disarmed,
Conquered, occurred, deferred, defeated,
Falling tears, more "champers-me-dears" downed.
Barbequed chicken, spare ribs, sausages, potatoes,
Salad, days back again, tactfully remain,
Kept plain, want to do it all again,
Acceptable, delectable confectionary,
Tasteful hide and seek from the big ogre,
Scared laughter, wanting more for sure.
Up for it, adds to kinship, friendship, relation,
More mature now I'm a blazing paradigm,
Grown up at last, surprising, to the test conquest,
Love, goodbyes, see you soon, keep in touch much.

GOT TECHNICAL

Had to check all my settings before writing –
A jinx had upset my normal ways,
I had to manually double-check the work,
Resetting obvious format text type,
Paragraph editing, spelling underlining,
Centring, conforming, reviewing editor,
Spellchecker got me under a spell.
Can't for a toffee, double checking,
Chicken licking, front bearing the brunt,
Double or bust at my cost,
A technical rebel, a bit fickle,
Comprise, despise malaise,
Venture fourth or fifth, sixish,
Wrapped up in bilingual,
Tangential, tantric deficit,
Comprising of who-done-it,
Got away with murder – not proud
Of being allowed to get away with
Being a naughty boy, cheeky monkey.
Blame it on my parents' deliverance,
Larkin said your parents "Fuck You Up!"
He was right, condoning, leave me alone.

START ANEW

Afresh, accomplished, achieving a polished
Diadem for recruiting a suitable employee,
To tender a reminder so as not to forget to
Apply for prescriptive, directive enabling.
Subversive subjects subjectively to
Announce the trouncing putting down
Of beleaguered, besieged benefactors,
Who want to benefit from unbelievable
Assumptions henceforth declared, compared,
By an assailant compere who dares to invigilate;
Monitoring, castigating regulations for a said,
Revoking disliking, disposing of the unwanted.
Flagrant infatuating attendees attending,
Symbiotic syllabuses symbolising aggrandising,
Magnifying the aforesaid dissolution, disabled
Parliament dissolved, general election forthwith,
Counting the votes, anecdotes, tales of woe,
In effect, deliberating discontinuing, ceasing,
The aforesaid format assails, invigilating,
Forthwith supervising a recruitment drive,
To undertake the following unreservedly.

APPARENTLY

By Apparitor AP Prior

Apparently, I am used to making things apparent,
Not stating the obvious, obliviously currently,
Concurrently alongside parallels juxtaposed,
I am a parent of two lads definitely,
Apparently, they deeply resemble moi,
Definitely show my traits, apparently good and bad.
Happy-sad parent, always there apparently,
I call a witness to account for apparent actions;
Currently conducted orchestrated fiddles,
Apparent riddles ostensible, sensible, apparent
Apparitions deluding my approach, apparently,
Seemingly apparent, deficient of differences
That definitely add up to a deficiency, apparently,
Of over-elaborating apparent apparitions, dispelling
All appendages that apparently actually apply to
My benefit; should I apply for an apparent loan,
Don't condone said apparitions of a ghostly nature
That apparently delude my good sense of apparent,
Realistic, venture forth apparently into full appraisal.

BEING LONELY

At first, too much space,
Collect thoughts, mind expands,
Think into sobriety sensibly,
Not letting broadness worry me,
Space has grace passionately,
Must conserve energy, parody,
Dismiss contradictory release from
Having to comply with statutory,
Legal jargon dismissively, apparently,
Deceptively delusional, illusional,
Conceptual, affirmative directly,
Too direct has the wrong effect.
I want to be right, polite, contrite,
Repent, lose the argument, amend,
Soft touch, friendly, bendy,
Malleable, convivial, dependable,
Giving expectant repentant,
Regretful, remorseful, sorry;
Won't do that again assuredly,
Refrain from upsetting, belittling,
Keeping good company comfortably.

RAISE MY GAME

Must pick myself up from being low,
Don't let the buggers grind you down,
Some people don't know they're doing it,
Have an opinion of you that's final.
Know what they think, you shrink,
Attitude on the blink, can't think
What to say about controversy;
If they knew me better, generous, delirious,
Uphill battle lost, rattle non-descript depict,
Have to outwit with a jealous, superior demeanour.
Contrary to the country, what country?
Are they from a diddle-dum conundrum?
I take it on the chin, chin-up chuck,
Grinders are reminders of blinders,
Supercilious, condescending, unhappy,
Something's unforgiveable, derisory,
Comprising, riding my luck pluck,
Good fortune must have come my way.
Have to say, make your own good fortune,
Not always understood in the hood,
For the greater good, got misunderstood,
Don't complain; raise my game.

ALGORITHM

Mathematical problem-solving,
A system that applies, resolves,
By rank, top page order, multitudes of
Bubbles rise to the top, sort out,
Merge loosely, stable match,
Organise popular reactions,
Partner-compatible material,
Join characteristics, solutions,
Easy potentialities form,
Possible potential,
Calculate output,
The shortest route,
Solving better,
More efficient,
Best characteristic,
Random chaos,
Holistic posture,
Benefits collective,
Solutions pleasing,
Learning mechanises,
MRI scan,
Preferences alike,
Find illustrating,

Estimated items,
Categories control,
Self-deprecating,
Analysis wayward,
Potential proliferates,
Preferences predominate,
Encapsulates, captures,
Calculate other,
Entrance, difference,
Enhanced conclusion,
Sold on sale,
Items overbought,
Solving best buy,
Matters, material,
Blocks replicate,
Accumulate the same,
Multiply multiples,
Compartmental parts,
The same but different.

QUAKER

I hardly use my mobile phone,
Don't drive a car, just a passenger,
Cycle to the village, out of touch
With modern life, my plight is strife.
Get other people to do jobs for me,
It's difficult to comply with society's ways,
Being disabled, double-vision haze,
MS has given me unreliable, contrivable,
Happy, dysfunctional, dismissible,
As if a bind confined, not adhering
To society's normal ways, as if subnormal.
Fit in as best I can, also ran in the race,
Out of place, loss of face, no trace,
Commonplace when disabled, unable.
I am not a quaker but feel like one,
I must be a lateral thinker out of touch,
With society's other side, predominately
Correct while I defect, indiscriminately
Discriminated, not understanding, pedantic,
Romantic, frantic, disabled disbeliever.
Contriver, reliable, defying all odds against me.

Author Anthony P Prior
who is disabled with MS.

Ingram Content Group UK Ltd.
Milton Keynes UK
UKHW020805310523
422626UK00011B/253